Ethical Diplomacy And The Trump Administration

Charles Ray

North Potomac, MD

Printed in the United States of America

Cover design and interior art by the author.

For use of this work in educational programs, contact the author at

charlesray.author@gmail.com or charlesray.author@yahoo.com

Other books by this author can be seen at:

https://charlesray-author.com

ISBN-13 9781082451683:

DEDICATION

To diplomats of all nationalities who labor, often anonymously and under hazardous condition, on behalf of their governments and the citizens of their countries. People who receive little or no thanks for the things they do for us on a daily basis, but who are soundly blamed whenever things go wrong.

CONTENTS

ACKNOWLEDGMENTS

The list of people who, directly and indirectly, contributed to this work is far too long to be included here, but I would like to single out one individual who played a significant role in getting me interested in the conduct of ethical diplomacy. Susan Johnson, President of the Association for Diplomatic Studies and Training (ADST), who was the president of the American Foreign Service Association (AFSA) in 2012 when I retired from the Foreign Service, who asked me to chair a Committee on Professionalism and Ethics for AFSA, an entity that was making great progress on developing an ethically-based professional code of conduct for the Foreign Service until a subsequent AFSA president disbanded it for reasons that are still unclear. It was Susan's abiding interest in putting the US diplomatic service on a sound ethical footing that sparked my interest in a subject that I've been studying and lecturing on ever since. .

"An ambassador is an honest man sent to lie
abroad for the good of his country."
(Legatus est vir bonus peregre missus ad
mentiendum rei publicae causa)

Ethical Diplomacy – What is it, and Why Does it Matter?

In 1604, while on a diplomatic assignment in Augsburg, the English diplomat and statesman, Sir Henry Wooten, wrote in a friend's album, "An ambassador is an honest man sent to lie abroad for the good of his country." In 1611, Caspar Schoppe, writing in a book slamming King James I and his reign, repeated this phrase in his effort to emphasize the lack of morals of James' administration. While Wooten, in defending himself, asserted that it was just a joke, James was not amused, and Wooten didn't receive another diplomatic assignment for many years. While the English version of Wooten's note can be interpreted in more than one way, the use of the Latin *mentiendum* (which means to lie, tell a falsehood) did not admit to any double meaning.

Unfortunately for today's diplomats, the negative meaning of Wooten's jocular note still holds. In many countries, foreign diplomats are viewed as spies for their governments, and are often treated accordingly. At home, especially in the United States, diplomats are given little thought, and considered by many to be spoiled dilettantes who spend their time attending cocktail parties and hobnobbing with foreigners on the taxpayer's dime. They have little to no idea what diplomats really do, basing their opinions on the biased and inaccurate portrayals in popular media.

This misapprehension of diplomacy and diplomats is not a modern phenomenon either. It is as old as the country itself. The United States was, at birth, suspicious of anything resembling what existed in the royal courts of Europe, having just obtained its independence from one of those empires, and refused to appoint ambassadors, associating with them with royalty. The new country sent ministers abroad as its senior representatives until the first ambassador was appointed in 1893, when the realization hit that a country with one of the world's richest economies and growing naval power could no longer be represented in foreign capitals by an individual who ranked in protocol order below the ambassadors of the smallest and poorest countries. Until the Foreign Service Act of 1924, known as the Rogers Act after its principal supporter in congress, John Jacob Rogers, U.S. representative from Massachusetts, the U.S. diplomatic and consular services (which until that time had been two separate services) were staffed by well-heeled, wealthy political appointees and business men with overseas connections and were politically connected to the administration in power. Only after 1924, when the two services were merged into the Foreign Service of the United States, did the country have career government employees staffing its embassies and consulates abroad.

The bias—even animus one might say—against diplomats and diplomacy came from, and still comes from, the highest officials. Thomas Jefferson, the principal drafter of the Declaration of Independence, who served as the nation's first secretary of state, from 1789 to 1794, once wrote that 'an independent America had no need of diplomats beyond a few commercial consuls.' That attitude has survived in one form or another down to the present day. Whenever there is a new administration at 1600 Pennsylvania Avenue, the last department to be considered, except when budget cuts are decided, is the oldest cabinet department, the Department of State.

If there is one thing I learned, though, in my thirty-plus years of service as an American diplomat, is that the image of a diplomat as someone who is less than honest, out of touch with the people of his or her own country, engaged in a never-ending round of social events is far from the reality. One of the most important traits of an effective diplomat is honesty and trust. Those to whom you report must trust your honesty or integrity, the foreigners you engage with in the performance of your duties must trust your honesty and integrity, and the American people, on whose behalf you're working in the first place, must trust your honesty and integrity. Get caught in a lie, and you lose that trust. Lose that trust and you cannot function effectively as a diplomat.

Diplomats can't always give a direct and truthful answer to a question: some things must be kept secret; but, withholding classified or sensitive information that is protected by law and regulation is not the same as lying. Later in this book I will discuss some ways this can be dealt with without crossing the line into lying.

Effective diplomats practice, whether or not they are aware of it, what I have chosen to call ethical diplomacy.

Just what is this ethical diplomacy? Finding a precise definition of the term is difficult for, while the

State Department's National Foreign Affairs Training Center (NAFTC), also known as the Foreign Service Institute (FSI), does offer courses in ethics, these focus on enforcement of ethics regulations which tell employees what *not* to do rather than what to do.

It might be helpful to start with what ethical diplomacy is not. It is not the 'moral diplomacy' proposed by U.S. President Woodrow Wilson in his 1912 election, a form of diplomacy in which we support only those countries whose moral beliefs are analogous to ours. This system of diplomacy was used by Wilson to support countries with democratic forms of government, and economically damage those with different ideologies. While Wilson's views have not shaped U.S. diplomacy as much as he might have wished, there remains a strain of this attitude in our foreign policy—tempered by the reality that circumstances often put us in the position of having to support or cooperate with non-democratic regimes in the interests of greater issues. During World War II, for example, we allied with and supported the communist Soviet Union in our fight against the Axis powers who were seen at the time as the greater threat. Our support and cozy relationship with Saudi Arabia, definitely a non-democratic country, is another case of reality taking precedence over moral considerations (in this case, in addition to Saudi oil, their support for our actions and policies in the Middle East have a higher priority for senior policy makers than their terrible human rights record, or the Wahabi sect's support of extremist groups worldwide). A study of world events since 1912, and the U.S. reaction to those events will reveal that Wilson's 'moral diplomacy' never had a chance of succeeding.

So, just to be clear, when I talk about ethical diplomacy, I am not talking about 'moral' diplomacy, although, an ethical diplomat has a strong moral core. Those morals, though, are not the patronizing morals of past centuries, with people of European descent believing that they and their culture were superior, and others should be happy to emulate them. They are the morals that recognize the innate dignity of every human being, but at the same time humans are not infallible, morals that recognize and abide by universally accepted principles, such as respect for human rights, respect for rule of law, etc. My study of how Wilson and his contemporaries applied moral diplomacy reveals a tendency to categorize countries, cultures and people as 'us' versus 'them,' or 'good' versus 'bad,' with 'us' being 'good' and 'them' being 'bad.' There was also a tendency, even with our putative allies, to be dismissive or patronizing with those who, though possessing democratic governments of a sort, didn't quite measure up to our economic or social level.

ETHICAL DIPLOMACY vs. WOODROW WILSON'S 'MORAL' DIPLOMACY	
ETHICAL	MORAL
- Based on universal values - Recognizes basic dignity of all	- Us vs. Them - Confrontational - Requires moral compromise

In defining ethical diplomacy, I would like to start by defining its component parts and related words and phrases.

Diplomacy: The art or practice of conducting international relations.

Ethics: The study of the general nature of morals and the specific moral choices an individual makes in relating to others; the rules or standards of conduct governing the members of a profession.

Ethical: Conforming to accepted principles of right and wrong that govern a profession.
(Source: *Webster's II New College Dictionary*

From the foregoing I then define ethical diplomacy as the 'conduct of international relations in conformity with accepted principles of right and wrong. I hasten to add, this is *my* definition, not one that is generally accepted. It will, however, help the reader to understand the content of this volume.

> # Ethical Diplomacy
>
> # The conduct of international relations conforming to accepted principles of right and wrong

Why is ethical diplomacy important? It's important for the reason I stated early in this chapter; in order to be effective, a diplomat must be trusted, and conducting oneself in accordance with universally accepted principles of right and wrong help to establish the diplomat as a person of integrity. Unfortunately, in the pursuit of national interests, governments have been known to lie, even the government of the U.S.A., and such mendacity is not limited to the domestic arena. Governments are amoral, and act to deceive in foreign policy as well sometimes. Unfortunately, the average person is incapable of distinguishing between foreign policy and diplomacy, and when they observe dishonorable behavior on the part of those making the policy, they tar the practitioners in the field with the same brush.

Governments are by their nature amoral, and while this does not excuse outright lying, current events amply demonstrate that some government officials have a very loose relationship with truth. Alternate facts, other people's truth, evasions, and blatant lies seem to be the order of the day in both domestic and foreign affairs.

The behavior of the Trump Administration, with

a president who has publicly told not a few, but thousands of lies since taking office in January 2017, complicates life for American diplomats in ways unlike any ever seen before. Pulling out of alliances, insulting traditional allies, and embracing adversaries, are all actions that place obstacles in the way America's representatives around the globe, and it is, in my opinion, only if ethical diplomacy is practiced assiduously, that we can minimize the danger being done to the image of the United States globally.

The question that must be asked, though: is this: is ethical diplomacy even possible in such a situation?

I have been interested in ethics in government service for a long time, so when I retired from the Foreign Service in 2012, and was asked by Susan Johnson, then president of the American Foreign Service Association (AFAA) to chair a professionalism and ethics committee (PEC), I jumped at the chance. One of the goals of the committee was to establish a code of professional conduct for the Foreign Service, based on agreed-upon core values of its members.

The PEC, with the assistance of the Institute of Government Ethics (IGE) conducted a survey of 1,300 members of the Foreign Service (officer and specialist, all ranks, overseas and domestic assignments, and all career fields) from April 19 to May 8, 2013 regarding beliefs, attitudes and values they associate with ethical decision making in the Foreign Service. From this survey, four core values were identified:

Honesty

Responsibility

Fairness

Respect

These were the values identified by more than two-third of all respondents regardless of rank, assignment, or career specialty.

The Department of State, in its annual financial and performance report, and the little-known FSO Presidential Commission (FSO/PC) publish core values, but the majority of the respondents to our survey were even aware of them. Only some 20% were aware of the State Department's core values: Loyalty, Character, Service, Accountability, Community, and Diversity, and only 13% knew of the FSO/PC's three core values: Integrity, Prudence and Ability. I, for one, was even unaware of the existence of the FSO/PC until I read the report of the survey, and only vaguely recalled having glanced at that section of an annual State Department financial report a time or two during my thirty-year career.

While I cannot be absolutely certain, I believe the lack of familiarity with these two slightly differing sets of core values is due to the fact that they were bureaucratically developed and pushed down into the workforce instead of doing as the ethics experts at IGE recommend, developing the core values identified by the rank and file members of the organization.

Organizational codes of conduct, according to IGE, include in their preamble the core values of the organization. Those values, as well as the code itself, should be the product of a cross section of the organization, representing the range of ranks, positions, and interests of the organization. Values that are bureaucratically forced on an organization from the top rather than produced from the membership, tend to be legalistic and compliance oriented, while those created by members of an organization are mainly aspirational or a combination of aspirational and compliance. In other words, bureaucratic values are of the 'what not to do' variety, while member-derived aspirational values are 'who we are and what we'd like to be.'

The diplomatic service of the United States, the U.S. Foreign Service, does not have a formal code of conduct, a situation that, in my opinion, ill equips it to deal with the disruption and ethical dilemmas that inevitably come with any change of political administration. Dedicated, loyal, and hard-working, Foreign Service Officers and Specialists, along with their civil service colleagues here in the United States, and the local staff (known as Locally Employed Staff, or LES) overseas manage nevertheless to do their jobs with integrity and dignity, protecting and advancing the nation's interests, looking out for American citizens abroad in a variety of ways, and maintaining the relationships that have contributed to our national security, even when the sometimes misguided actions of politicians have pushed things in the wrong direction. They have effectively explained inflammatory, sometimes insulting, statements and actions, and kept our international relations moving in a generally positive direction.

The situation diplomats face with the current administration, however, is unlike any other in the nation's history. Even the isolationist fervor of the period preceding World War II pales in comparison.

In the following chapter, I will offer my assessment of this administration and the challenges it presents. I would caution the reader to keep in mind that these are my personal opinions. They do nor represent the views of any organization, government or non-government, but are meant to inspire thought and discussion of the future of American diplomacy in and beyond the current administration.

"I play to people's fantasies. People may not always think big themselves, but they can still get excited by those who do. That's why a little hyperbole never hurts. People want to believe that something is the biggest and the greatest and the most spectacular." – Donald J. Trump in 'The Art of The Deal.'

Cutting Deals – The Story of Donald Trump

When Donald J. Trump, real estate mogul and reality TV personality, announced his candidacy for president in 2016, no one in either party, the media, or the public really took him seriously. Had they bothered to carefully read his best-selling book, *The Art of the Deal*, they might have viewed his actions a bit differently, and a lot more seriously.

For starters, it would have been useful not just to read the book, but to learn its history. Co-authored by Tony Schwartz and published in 1987 by Random House, it was part memoir, part business how-to book, and was an instant best-seller. It brought Trump something he craves above many things – national name recognition. Schwartz was hired to work with him on the book in 1985, but in 2016, after multiple public claims by Trump that *he* wrote it, claims that Trump actually wrote none of it, and only removed a few critical references to colleagues after he (Schwartz) had finished writing it based upon many interviews with Trump, as well as being allowed to listen in on his phone calls. This assertion has also been supported by the book's publisher, Howard Kaminsky.

For his part, since this astonishing revelation, Trump has given conflicting responses. On one occasion, he'd hired Schwartz from among many choices to write the book, and on another claiming that Schwartz didn't write the book but that he (Trump) did.

To add further drama to the saga of *The Art of The Deal*, in a 2019 interview on CNN, Schwartz described Trump as a sociopath who has no feelings for others.

During the 2016 presidential campaign, many of Trump's actions were right out of *The Art of the Deal*, while others, during the campaign and since, were in direct contradiction to the book.

In the previous chapter I stated that every new administration in the White House brings a certain degree of disruption to the work of American diplomats at home and abroad. But the Trump Administration, in my opinion, has raised the disruption factor to a level that I've not seen during my entire fifty-year government career; disruption that not only complicates life for those who must represent U.S. interests abroad, but that create confusion for our allies, damage the U.S. image and our credibility worldwide, and make the world a less safe and hospitable place for us now and in the future.

The Border Wall and the Muslim Ban – *Build the Wall!*

Immigration has long been a sensitive and complex

issue for the U.S. Government, driven by domestic political considerations, but with international implications. Not since the Page Act of 1875, prohibiting Chinese women from immigrating to the United States, and the Chinese Exclusion Act of 1882, banning immigration of Chinese laborers, has there been such intensity in restricting entry into the U.S. of specific national ethnic groups as we've seen since 2017.

Of the many promises Donald Trump made during the 2016 campaign, two that have been at the forefront of much of his rhetoric and actions since his inauguration have been the building of a wall on the southern border and a ban on issuance of visas to people from Muslim countries.

The border wall grew out of his campaign handlers desire to get a candidate who hates to read or get briefings, to remember to mention immigration, a key issue for the GOP, especially when addressing its base. Figuring that Trump, a real estate developer, would relate easily to a construction related mnemonic, they suggested he talk about building a wall on the border to control illegal immigration. The image resonated with many at his campaign events, leading to chants of 'Build the Wall!'. A man who feeds off the adoration of an audience, he then made this a central issue, and the complex problem of illegal immigration and immigration reform was reduced to the simple formula, "I will build a great, great wall on our southern border, and I will make Mexico pay for that wall. Mark my words." His first proposal envisioned a 1,000-mile stretch of wall along the 1,900-mile border.

Of course, once in office, reality set in. He had no way of making Mexico pay for a wall—the Mexicans have remained adamant that they will *not* pay. For a man who claims to be a master negotiator, the way he dealt with Mexico on this issue is, to say the least, strange.

First, he insulted the government and people, when he accused the Mexicans of not sending their best to the U.S., but instead sending rapists, criminals, and drug dealers. "And some, I assume, are good people," he said, almost as an afterthought.

Despite his trade war with China, he accused Mexico of 'ripping of the US almost more than any other nation, making millions on our bad trade deals and the remittances sent by illegal immigrants in the US.

If your aim is to gain the cooperation of your negotiating partner, and as he promised his base in this case, get that partner to 'pick up the tab' for your project, hurling insults seems counterproductive. Our diplomats in Mexico, I have no doubt, have been experiencing many uncomfortable exchanges with the host government since 2016.

Of course, if you read another of Trump's books, *Think Big*, it begins to make sense. Donald Trump is a zero-sum negotiator. He does not seek a win-win outcome in negotiations. In his own words, "You hear lots of people say that a great deal is when both sides win. That's a bunch of crap. In a great deal you win— not the other side.

The Real Wall.

On a domestic note, having failed to obtain funding for his 1,000-mile wall when Republicans controlled both houses of congress, Trump got into a stare-down with House Speaker Nancy Pelosi after the 2018 mid-term elections gave control of the House of Representatives to the Democrats, bragging that he'd 'be proud to shut the government down for border security.' The stand-off resulted in the longest partial shutdown of the U.S. Government in history, with over 800,000 federal workers and thousands of contract workers either furloughed without pay or ordered to work without pay for over a month (two pay periods). The ironic thing is that many of the workers affected by the shutdown were the very people charged with border security, along with the departments of State and Justice. The president's own Secret Service protection detail had to work without pay for a month.

Smackdown!

When the shutdown finally ended with a three-week continuing resolution, the president still didn't have the money for his wall, the economy had lost billions, and the cost of replacing those workers who said 'enough is enough,' and left government for civilian sector jobs has yet to be calculated.

The REAL National Emergency.

The Muslim ban is another campaign promise designed to appeal to the fears and prejudices of that fringe element of support known as the 'base.' Fear, distrust, and loathing of the 'other,' as evidenced by anti-Chinese sentiment at the turn of the century, anti-Japanese sentiment after Pearl Harbor, and Islamophobia in the wake of the September 11, 2001 terrorist attacks, seems to lurk just beneath the surface of the American body politic. Trump capitalized on this tendency in his campaign, helped by mass shooting at an Orlando, Florida night club on June 12, 2016, when x killed 49 people and injured 53 before being killed by police, citing this as an example of how terrorists used the immigration system to do their dirty work. The thing that his unquestioning supporters failed to understand was that the shooter, a 29-year-old security guard, whose parents came from Afghanistan, was himself born in New York, and had lived in the U.S. his entire life.

Such details, though, seem to have no relevance when it comes to Trump's promises to his base. Within days of assuming office, he issued Executive Order 13769, Protecting the Nation from Foreign Terrorist Entry into the United States, which was effective January 27, 2017 until it was struck down by a federal judge on Marcy 6, 2017. In addition to limiting refugee numbers and other restrictions, it essentially placed a ban on issuance of visas to people coming from Iran, Iraq, Somalia, Sudan, Syria, and Yemen, all predominantly Muslim countries. While the White House tried after an international and domestic outcry, to paint the order as 'not a Muslim ban,' the president's own rhetoric made it abundantly clear that it was in fact just that.

There were a number of problems with the order, whether or not it was acknowledged a ban on Muslims. In the first instance, Trump's own Department of Homeland Security (DHS) stated that the seven countries on the list posed no terror risk. Additionally, more than a half of the people the government had determined were inspired to carry out attacks on American soil were born in the United States, and the rest came from 26 countries, and only two of the countries on the 'banned' list were in that group. The list did not include Saudi Arabia (where most of the 9/11 hijackers came from), Egypt (home of the Muslim Brotherhood), Pakistan, or Afghanistan. The latter two countries had provided safe haven to terrorists such as Osama bin Laden, and have significant problems with extremist groups.

Imagine being an American diplomat serving abroad when that executive order was published, and having to try and explain the rationale behind it.

Backing out of treaty commitments – *pactus interruptus*

Along with honesty, diplomats and the nations they represent are judged by their reliability. Once a commitment is made, will it be kept, or will it be abandoned for something better? With the exception of the feeling of abandonment of many of our Southeast Asian allies after we pulled out of Vietnam, the United

States has, since World War II, been seen as a reliable ally. We could be depended upon to take a leadership role in addressing the pressing, and sometimes existential, problems facing the globe, whether it was protecting the environment or fighting human trafficking.

Since January 2017, though, we have walked away from one commitment after another.

The Paris Climate Accord. On June 1, 2017, less than five months after taking office, Trump announced that the United States would withdraw from the Paris Climate Accord, despite intense pressure from business executives, other world leaders, and his own daughter, citing the accord as an 'American job killer and a way for other nations to take advantage of the United States.' The agreement, which went into effect in November 2016, is aimed at preventing increases in global temperature by gradually reducing man-made emissions linked to rising temperatures, and keep the Earth from warming by more than 3.6 degrees Fahrenheit. Trump's predecessor, former President Barack Obama had made a non-binding pledge to participate in the accord, promising to lower American emissions by 26-28 percent by 2025, and promised $3 billion to the UN Green Climate Fund. In his statement announcing the withdrawal, Trump said he'd be open to renegotiating certain aspects of the agreement, but France, Germany, and Italy gave him the thumbs down, saying that the agreement was a cornerstone in agreement among nations and it 'could not be renegotiated.'

The Trans-Pacific Partnership (TPP). On his first day in office, Trump signed an executive order pulling the United States out of the Trans-Pacific Partnership (TPP), declaring keeping his campaign promise to pull out was a 'great thing for the American worker. The pact, a 12-nation trade deal that included the U.S., Japan, Mexico, Canada, Australia, New Zealand,

Vietnam, Chile, Peru, Malaysia, Singapore, and Brunei. It was negotiated during the Obama Administration, but had never been ratified by congress. Economic analysis of the deal showed that it would have positively contributed to American economic growth, and moreover, would have enhanced American influence in Asia and the world by reassuring friend and foe alike that the U.S. is a contributing global power. Pulling out increased uncertainty among our allies on both economic and foreign policy matters, and was the first time the U.S. had withdrawn from an agreement that it had championed. Trump's stated policy was that the U.S. would negotiate trade agreements with countries individually.

The North American Free Trade Agreement (NAFTA). During the 2016 presidential campaign, Trump made clear his disdain for multilateral trade agreements with did not, in his view, 'benefit the United States, and a decided preference for bilateral trade agreements. In addition to the TPP, one agreement he singled out as being 'unfair' to the U.S. was the NAFTA, the three-way agreement among the U.S., Canada, and Mexico. Trump has on more than one occasion threatened to pull out of NAFTA. So far, he has not done so, but his administration did negotiate a new trilateral agreement; on November 30, 2018, the three countries signed the United States-Mexico-Canada Agreement (USMCA), which has yet to be ratified by congress, and which Trump has hailed as better than NAFTA (which, by the way, is still in effect). Confusing? Imagine being an American diplomat trying to explain this situation to a foreign audience. In all fairness, there are parts of the USMCA that improve NAFTA; but each also has a downside that the administration fails to point out. For example, USMCA requires that auto companies must manufacture at least 75 percent of a car's components in one of the three countries, where NAFTA only required 62.5 percent. It also requires at least 30 percent of the car to be made by workers earning at least $16 per hour, increasing to 40 percent in 2023. Autos not meeting these requirements will be subject to tariffs. While these changes *should* create more jobs for U.S. auto workers, it *could* also reduce U.S. jobs related to cars sold in China, because the higher labor costs will make them too expensive for the Chinese market. With China on the way to eventually becoming the world's largest economy, that is a problem lurking down the road for the U.S. economy.

The Intermediate-Range Nuclear Force (INF) Treaty. The Intermediate-Range Nuclear Forces (INF) Treaty, also known as the Treaty Between the United States of America and the Union of Soviet Socialist Republics on the Elimination of Their Intermediate-Range and Shorter-Range Missiles, was signed by U.S. President Ronald Reagan and Soviet President Mikhail Gorbachev on December 8, 1987. It was ratified by the U.S. Senate on May 27, 1988, and went into effect on June 1. The treaty eliminated all land-based ballistic and cruise missiles with ranges from 310 to 3,420 miles. It did not cover air- or sea-launched missiles. By May 1991, 2,692 missiles had been eliminated, and a ten-year period of on-site verification inspections began. On October 20, 2018, Donald Trump announced that the U.S. was withdrawing from the treaty due to Russia's non-compliance, and formally suspended the treaty on February 1, 2019. Russia, citing the U.S. withdrawal, suspended its participation in the treaty on the following day. Negotiation of the INF Treaty took seven years, and despite Russian cheating, it contributed to the end of the Cold War and ushered in decades of strategic stability. With George W. Bush pulling the U.S. out of the Anti-Ballistic Missile Treaty in 2001, and the New START Treaty set to expire in 2021, the world will be left without any limits on the nuclear arsenals of the two main nuclear powers for the first time since 1972. In addition, other countries, such as China, are likely to look to increase their own arsenals, creating the specter of a global nuclear arms race.

Disrupting traditional Alliances - *Keep Enemies Close, Drive Friends Away*

At some point in a diplomatic career, every diplomat is likely to be called in by his or her host government to explain a statement by a politician that was made for domestic consumption, but was deemed an insult to the host. Even more problematic is when a diplomat has to try and explain statements that are seen as siding with or giving aid and comfort to an adversary. During my thirty years as a diplomat, though, I've not seen the frequency of such instances that have occurred since 2017

"That's my boy!"

Actually, the attacks on friends and neighbors started during the campaign, with Trump accusing Mexico of 'taking our money and sending us drugs.'

Since, the inauguration, though, no one—save a few of the world's dictatorships like Russia and Saudi Arabia—has been spared. Even long-standing allies like the UK, Canada, and Australia have felt the sharp edge of Trump's tongue as he relentlessly pursues his 'America first' policy, even if it means dismantling long-standing alliances. At the annual NATO summit in July 2018, he accused Germany of being a 'captive of Russia,' called the NATO member states 'delinquent' in their defense spending, and insisted that they immediately increase the percentage of GDP devoted to defense.

Some of his vitriolic rhetoric in regard to allies and trade partners are self-immolation. For instance, during trade talks with the Canadians, in a White House meeting that was off the record, but leaked anyway, Trump reportedly called the Canadians weak and said that the upcoming trade deal would be totally on U.S. terms. At the 2018 UN General Assembly, Trump further insulted our closest neighbor by ignoring the Canadian prime minister's attempt to say hello, and then not standing when he finally shook hands with him as he'd done with other leaders. Later, Trump said that he'd rejected a Canadian request for a one-on-one meeting between him and Prime Minister Justin Trudeau because the Canadians had 'treated us badly.' Trudeau later said that he'd never sought a meeting.

In contrast to Trump's brusque, often personal maltreatment of allies, he has been eerily solicitous of the feelings of countries that are our adversaries, or countries, like Saudi Arabia, who have checkered human rights records.

The strangest, and in many ways most dangerous, of these relationships, and one that seems to be at the root of many of the problems plaguing Trump's Administration, is the one he has with Russian president Vladimir Putin (See the cartoon on the previous page). His steadfast refusal to directly impugn Putin for Russian interference in the 2016 elections (as well as elections before and after 2016), despite the credible evidence presented by the U.S. intelligence and law enforcement community that they did, is inexplicable. Knowledgeable people are still scratching their heads over his statement in Helsinki, after a meeting with Putin, when he said, in effect, 'the U.S. intelligence community says Russia hacked our election, but President Putin strongly denies it, and I see no reason why they should have done it.' He later tried to walk the "see no reason why they should have done,' it by saying he meant to say 'no reason why they should *not* have done it,' but that horse was already out of the barn.

Trump, in remarks at the White House in late 2018, voiced the Russian propaganda line about why the Soviets went into Afghanistan; 'they were there because of a terrorist threat.,' and said they were 'right' to be there. I have yet to hear an attempt to explain that historical and political faux pas.

While no one has yet come up with a credible explanation for Trump's apparent fascination with and subservience to Vladimir Putin, other than his admiration for strong men, his bromance with Saudi Arabia seems clear—all evidence indicates that it's motivated by money. He and the Trump organization have engaged in business dealings with the Saudis since the 1990s, and among the many high-paying guests in his hotel properties, especially the Trump Hotel in Washington, DC, the Saudi Arabians are included. His first trip abroad as president was on May 20, 2017, and it was to Saudi Arabia, where he was praised and feted by the Saudi royals. When Saudi exile Jamal Khashoggi, a *Washington Post* correspondent, was killed in the Saudi Arabian consulate in Istanbul, Turkey, the Saudis at first denied it, then issued conflicting accounts of what happened, and then finally, admitted the killing, but said it had been a group of 'rogue' Saudi security officers. Despite U.S. intelligence assessments that it is highly likely Saudi crown prince Mohamed bin Salman was not only aware of the murder, but directed it, Trump has failed to explicitly condemn the action, and has appeared to accept the Saudi version of events over his own intelligence officials.

Finally, there is the complicated relationship with the dictatorial and reclusive regime of Kim Jong-un of the Democratic People's Republic of Korea (DPRK). The problem of a nuclear North Korea has plagued every American president since 1962, when it began a policy of hyper-militarization. The country requested Soviet assistance in building nuclear weapons, but indications are the Soviets refused, instead offering to help North Korea develop a peaceful nuclear energy program. North Korea's Yongbyon Nuclear Scientific Research Center was completed in 1965, and the country began its weapons program in the 1980s. In 1985, North Korea ratified the Non-Proliferation Treaty (NPT) but did not include the required safeguards until 1992. When the International Atomic Energy Agency (IAEA) attempted to verify North Korea's guarantees in 1993, the agency was not allowed to conduct a special inspection. The IAEA reported this noncompliance to the UN Security Council. North Korea announced its withdrawal from the NPT, but then suspended that withdrawal before it took effect. The U.S. response to North Korea's activities was in the form of the 1994 Agreed Framework, wherein the U.S. agreed to facilitate the supply of two light water reactors in exchange for the country's disarmament. Implementation of the Agreed Framework was difficult from the start, and it fell apart in 2002, the same year that Pakistan admitted that the DPRK had gained access to Pakistan's nuclear technology in the late 1990s. In 2003, North Korea again announced its withdrawal from the NPT, and in 2005, admitted that it had nuclear weapons. The first supposedly successful test of a nuclear weapon was on October 9, 2006, and the following January, North Korea confirmed that it had nuclear weapons. The next international effort to denuclearize the Korean Peninsula was the Six-Party Talks in 2003, which included North Korea, South Korea, China, Russia, Japan, and the United States. The North Koreans promised to shut down their main reactor at Yongbyon, which was confirmed by the IAEA, but when North Korea launched a satellite in 2009, the Six-Party Talks, like the Agreed Framework, fell apart. From 2009, North Korea began a series of weapons tests, many announced to the world by North Korean state television, and by April 2009, the country was considered a "nuclear power,' by most in the international community. These activities triggered international sanctions, which caused an on-again, off-again status of the country's weapons testing.

In addition to sanctions, including UN sanctions, the U.S. approach to the issue was primarily diplomatic until after Trump's 2017 inauguration. Almost immediately, he started a war of fiery rhetoric with North Korea, promising 'fire and fury' should the reclusive nation 'act unwisely.' The North Koreans responded in kind, including testing a rocket that had the range to reach U.S. territory in the Pacific. The escalating 'war of words' ratcheted up tensions and uncertainty in the region and internationally, but especially in South Korea and Japan, both within range of North Korea's tactical short- and medium-range nukes, as well as its conventional forces. The verbal standoff lasted until North Korea's Kim agreed to a summit with Trump in Singapore in June 2018, which resulted in an inconclusive 'agreement,' which Trump hailed as 'ending the nuclear threat on the Korean Peninsula.' Trump unilaterally suspended joint

US-South Korean military exercises, using the North Korean propaganda term, 'war games,' and praised Kim for his 'leadership.' In early 2019, U.S. and international intelligence agencies were in agreement that the North Koreans had not, in fact, given up their nuclear weapons, and showed no signs of doing so. Trump's response to this was to contradict and chide his own intelligence chiefs, and announce another summit with Kim that was held in late February 2019, this time in Hanoi, Vietnam. No deal was reached at that meeting, and Trump abruptly walked out. He then scheduled another meeting with Kim, this time in South Korea, at Panmunjom on the demarcation line between the two Koreas. At this meeting, which also resulted in no tangible progress in dismantling North Korea's nuclear program, Trump took the unprecedented step of stepping across the demarcation line and entering North Korea, the first sitting U.S. President to do so. While this was an historic event, it still made no progress in the main objective of curbing Kim Jong-un's nuclear weapons program, and a subsequent announcement that US-South Korea military exercises would take place resulted in the North Koreans announcing that they were considering reneging on previous verbal commitments Kim made to Trump, and pointing out that there has been no formal written commitment for North Korea to do anything.

At this writing, the situation on the Korean Peninsula is still in flux, we are coming dangerously close to direct hostilities between the US and Iran in the Straits of Hormuz, and thanks to leaked diplomatic cables written by the UK ambassador to the US in which he described the administration as dysfunctional and the president as impulsive, inept, and incompetent, relations with one of our oldest allies are strained. We still face the prospect of Russian—and other foreign actors—maliciously interfering in our electoral process, and the administration doesn't appear to take this threat seriously, which undermines our programs to encourage countries in transition to hold free and fair elections.

Hook, line, and stinker – a strange bromance.

"Whatever is my right as a man is also the right of another, and it becomes my duty to guarantee as well as to possess." – Thomas Paine, Rights of Man

Is Ethical Diplomacy Possible Under the Current Administration?

Whenever the occupant at 1600 Pennsylvania Avenue changes, American diplomats, at home and in the field, have to make some adjustments, even when the new occupant is from the same party as the outgoing chief executive—although, that hasn't happened often in the past several decades, and when there is a change in political party, the changes tend to be more dramatic. For example, when the Clinton Administration was replaced by that of George W. Bush, and 'regime change' became the buzz word *du jour*, relationships between some of our diplomats and their host governments became quite touchy. Most of the changes that I observed during my thirty years of diplomatic service were more or less cosmetic, and really had only minimal impact on my ability to conduct diplomacy to achieve the foreign policy goals established by the politically-elected leadership.

For example, when the U.S. position on the International Criminal Court (ICC) involved the threat of withholding assistance from any country whose government did not agree to refrain from referring American citizens to the court, the aim was valid; there *was* the possibility that some countries would use the ICC as a propaganda weapon against the United States. The method, though, smacked of bullying, and in most cases unnecessary. In any event, in my own case, as U.S. ambassador to a small, strategically insignificant country that was not high on the interest list of most senior policymakers, I followed the technique I've heard veteran diplomat Tom Pickering express, 'not following the talking points verbatim,' and in my pitch to the government I stressed the valid reasons for the U.S. not being part of the ICC—the U.S. legal system prosecutes Americans who commit crimes against humanity anywhere in the world, and it would not be good for anyone if the U.S. was targeted for unfair treatment. The government was aware of the law and instructions, but, I believe, appreciated my not poking them in the eye with it, and signed the agreement immediately. I achieved the desired goal without using the bullying technique implied by the instructions.

For example, when the U.S. position on the International Criminal Court (ICC) involved the threat of withholding assistance from any country whose government did not agree to refrain from referring American citizens to the court, the aim was valid; there *was* the possibility that some countries would use the ICC as a propaganda weapon against the United States. The method, though, smacked of bullying, and in most cases unnecessary. In any event, in my own case, as U.S. ambassador to a small, strategically insignificant country that was not high on the interest list of most senior policymakers, I followed the technique I've heard veteran diplomat Tom Pickering express, 'not following the talking points verbatim,' and in my pitch to the government I stressed the valid reasons for the U.S. not being part of the ICC—the U.S. legal system prosecutes Americans who commit crimes against humanity anywhere in the world, and it would not be good for anyone if the U.S. was targeted for unfair treatment. The government was aware of the law and instructions, but, I believe, appreciated my not poking them in the eye with it, and signed the agreement immediately. I achieved the desired goal without using the bullying technique implied by the instructions.

The Trump Administration, though, presents a situation unlike anything I saw during over fifty years of government service (twenty years in the military and thirty-plus in the Foreign Service); something akin to what I observed as a teen during the fifties watching Senator Joe McCarthy on TV waving his 'lists' around and accusing government employees of being 'Red' spies. Many a government career during the 'Red Scare' period was destroyed because of activity or statements that were not in line with McCarthy's idea of 'American.'

From the outside I see what appears to be a similar situation with the Trump Administration. A Foreign Service Officer I met told me that in the State Department, for example, anyone pointing out that a set of talking points for a Department senior official contains factual errors, is apt to be accused of not being a 'team player.' The concept of 'alternative facts' as opposed to 'fact,' plain and simple, or 'truth,' seems to be the way things currently operate. Senior political officials make public statements containing errors or untruths, but are in line with the president's statements or position on an issue, and they go unchallenged except by some in the media, who are immediately labeled as purveyors of 'fake news.' Personal loyalty to the boss seems to be valued more than loyalty to the Constitution, and oaths of office are being rendered meaningless.

Even the most senior officials are not immune from such treatment. When the heads of the intelligence agencies, testifying before Congress, made statements about the Islamic State (IS), North Korea, and Iran, that contradicted statements Trump has made publicly, he publicly rebuked them, calling them 'naïve,' and stating that they needed to 'go back to school.' When senior political appointees of an administration receive such treatment for being true to the oath they took when they assumed office, one can only imagine what would happen to a career official who did the same.

For those who might not be familiar with the federal oath of office, it should be remembered that it is required by the Constitution, and enshrined in the U.S. legal code; 5 U.S.C. 3331 states, "An individual, except the President, elected or appointed to an office of honor or profit in the civil service or uniformed services shall take the following oath: 'I, (name of individual), do solemnly swear (or affirm) that I will support and defend the Constitution of the United States against all enemies, foreign and domestic; that I will bear true faith and allegiance to the same; that I take this obligation freely, without any mental reservation or purpose of evasion; and that I will well and faithfully discharge the duties of the office on which I am about to enter. So help me God.'" Employees fo the United States Government, including all members of Congress, are required to take this oath before assuming elected or appointed office. The oath taken by the president at his or her inauguration is contained in Article II, Section 1 of the U.S. Constitution:

"I do solemnly swear (or affirm) that I will faithfully execute the office of President of the United States, and will to the best of my ability, preserve, protect, and defend the Constitution of the United States."

Note that there is nothing in the oath that appointed or elected officials take that says they must be loyal to any individual, including the president. When I served in government, and the person above me was living up to his oath, and that includes the president, I had on problem with being loyal to him or her. Looking at the current situation from the comfortable perch of my retirement, though, I wonder if I would be able to say the same thing today, and can understand why so many senior career diplomats are resigning or retiring.

That, though, presents a very serious problem.

While changes in politically appointed positions is normal when there is a change in administrations, these changes are not always accompanied by the outgoing incumbents retiring or resigning, as has been the case with many of the senior State Department changes. The abrupt departure of so many senior people can (will, I predict) have a long-term negative impact on the Foreign Service, and on the ability to carry out effective diplomacy, for a long time to come.

The most immediate problem, and one that doesn't seem to trouble a White House that is more concerned with the opinions of rabid, right-wing radio and TV shock jocks than experienced professionals, is the loss of expert advice when dealing with foreign policy situations, such as IS and Syria or North Korean nuclear weapons.

The role that diplomats play in providing the channel for ongoing communications with foreign governments, especially our friends and allies, is undercut when the commander-in-chief is frequently making disparaging statements about those friends and allies, is not consulting them or his own senior officials when making key foreign policy decisions, or is publicly contradicting his diplomats and senior officials on a regular basis.

While a certain level of disruption is inevitable with a new administration, the level of disruption brought on by the administration that took office in 2017, apparently deliberate in some instances, is unprecedented, and, I predict, it will have an impact on our ability to conduct effective, ethical diplomacy for years to come, if not decades.

The Hollowing Out of American Diplomacy

The hemorrhage of senior diplomatic officials began within days of the beginning of the new administration, when, according to a January 25, 2017 *Washington Post* report, four of the State Department's top career officials submitted their 'resignations.' The four career Foreign Service Officers, who had served under both Democratic and Republic administrations, were the Undersecretary of Management, the Assistant Secretary of State for Administration, the Assistant Secretary of State for Consular Affairs, and the Director of the Office of Foreign Missions. These departures, which were described as 'routine' by the State Department spokesperson, but as 'forced resignations' by an unnamed department source, were just five days behind the retirements of the Assistant Secretary of State for Diplomatic Security and the Director of the Bureau of Overseas Building Operations. Together, these career officials represented over a century of collective experience. According to David Wade, who was the department's chief of staff when John Kerry was Secretary of State, this was the largest simultaneous departure of so many senior people that anyone could remember, and this much expertise—especially in security, management, and consular positions, which are difficult to find in the private sector—would be difficult to replace. It should be noted, too, that these departures took place before Rex Tillerson, the nominee for the Secretary of State position, had been confirmed by the Senate.

These departures were characterized by one senior department official as 'the White House cleaning house.' And, these were not the only troubling departures of senior expertise in areas critical to US national security, nor were they the only harbingers of trouble ahead for the country's diplomatic establishment and for the conduct of effective diplomacy.

In addition to the previously mentioned departures, there were a number of retirements and resignations of people from critical policy areas, some in protest against the new administration's policies, others, according to unnamed sources, because of pressure from the political leadership.

The numbers, provided by the Foreign Service's bargaining unit and professional association, the American Foreign Service Association (AFSA) in November 2017, indicate that from January to November 2017, the number of people in senior positions declined from around 15 percent for minister counselors (equivalent to two-star general rank in the military) and 42 percent for career ministers (equivalent to three-star rank). These are people who have spent twenty years or more in their careers, and their talents cannot be replaced overnight, nor can they be effectively replaced by political appointees from the private sector, many of whom have zero foreign policy experience before receiving their appointments.

As if that is not enough of a problem, under Trump's first secretary of state, Rex Tillerson, former CEO of Exxon, hiring was frozen, with the number of entry-level Foreign Service Officer hires down to 100 in 2017, compared to 366 in 2016. The administration's apparent lack of regard for the career diplomatic service even impacted applications, with the number of people registering to take the Foreign Service entrance exam dropping by more than half from 2016 to 2017.

Even lacking foreign policy experience, one would have expected a senior business leader like Tillerson to know better. If he'd done at Exxon what he did at the State Department; lose senior staff, not promote people to replace them, and not hire enough new people, the company would've suffered. It wouldn't have been able to perform its basic function particularly well, and he might well have been looking for a new job himself, which is what happened to him at State, although, not for what he'd done to the institution, but because of policy differences with his boss. His replacement, Mike Pompeo, reversed the hiring freeze, but has yet to replace the lost senior talent, so while a band-aid has been placed on the wound Tillerson inflicted, the illness has not been treated.

The degrading of capability at the Department of State has not been confined to the Foreign Service. In December 2016, there were 2,580 civil service employees at the Department of State in the foreign affairs occupation series. By September 2017, that number had dropped to 2,273, an approximate 12 percent decrease. Like their Foreign Service counterparts, the foreign affairs officers have years of experience, and provide advice, administration, and research in a broad range of foreign policy areas, and are often key figures in international negotiations.

During the first year of the administration, around 16 percent of the department's employees with 25 years or more of service departed, and were not replaced. When you consider that the State Department has to compete in the international diplomatic arena with countries represented by senior, experienced people, according to Ron Neumann, a retired Foreign Service Officer who served as ambassador three times, and is now president of the American Academy of Diplomacy, in an interview in the February 2018 issue of *The Atlantic*, "you're the high school kid trying to pretend you're in college."

Ethical Dilemmas over Policy Disagreement – Leave or Fight from the Inside?

Newly-hired Foreign Service Officers commit to a number of things, among them, the commitment to carry out the policies decided upon by the elected leadership to the best of their ability even when they disagree with those policies. Policy disagreements are usually relatively minor, such as the U.S. policy regarding membership in the International Criminal Court (ICC). The U.S. refused to join the ICC because of the fear that certain member countries would use the court as a propaganda tool against the U.S., and bring cases against U.S. officials or military personnel. A valid concern, but the approach the government took to address the issue; asking countries to sign an agreement not to refer American citizens to the ICC, or face a loss of U.S. aid; smacked of bullying, and had the potential to alienate countries that might otherwise be supportive.

At this time, I was ambassador to a Southeast Asian country with a small Muslim population, and in the immediate aftermath of the September 11 attacks, we could ill afford to alienate any country whose support we might need to address extremist groups. Thus, while I didn't disagree with the policy itself, I had issues with the way we were handling it. My oath, however, required that I carry out the policy to the best of my ability, which I did, by simply not referring to the threat of loss of assistance, but with a focus on the U.S. legal system and respect for rule of law, when I approached the host government. In doing this, I was following a practice I'd learned from a senior diplomat for whom I have the greatest respect; 'you don't always have to follow your talking points explicitly, as long as you get the desired outcome.'

What do you do, though, when you not only disagree with the tone of the policy, but find the policy itself morally repugnant?

Staying in the system and looking for ways to change the policy, while it sounds fine, can push you perilously close to the line of violating your oath of office and acting unethically. On the other hand, holding your nose and carrying out a policy that violates your own moral code, means sacrificing your integrity, and at that point, you're no longer practicing ethical diplomacy.

In my view, the only ethical thing to do in such a case is to resign or, if you're eligible, retire. You can then fight the policy ethically from outside the institution, as many Foreign Service professionals have been doing for decades, starting with mass resignations in protest of the Vietnam War, for example.

Leaving a job that you've devoted your life to, before you'd planned to leave, is never an easy thing to do. In addition to the emotional burden, for many, it can create financial hardship, with mortgages, educational expenses, and the like. I wish I could say that there's an easy answer to this, but there's not. This is a decision that a person must make without outside intervention—beyond consulting immediate family who will be impacted by it. The question that you must ask is this; can you live with sacrificing your integrity and self-respect if you do not do the honorable thing?

Since my retirement in 2012, I have been in contact with a number of still-serving Foreign Service Officers of all ranks and career fields. What I've been hearing from them since 2017 troubles me greatly.

I cling to the belief that ethical diplomacy is still

possible, primarily at the lower ranks of the service where officers operate out of the orbit of partisan political appointees, but I'm not so sanguine about the prospects for those at higher ranks. As I note in the following paragraph, acting on principle and trying to do what's 'right' risks being labeled as an outlier, and disloyal, and can have serious consequences on an individual's career.

At a social event in early 2019, for instance, I spoke with an FSO who serves as an office director in the Department of State. I was told by this officer that after pointing out some inconsistencies and outright falsehoods in a set of talking points being prepared for the Secretary of State, there followed an email accusing this officer (who I will not identify for obvious reasons) of not being a team player, and up to the time of our conversation, no more talking points had been sent for clearance.

This is troubling on a number of fronts. First, it is the duty of members of a staff to provide accurate information to their boss. I learned this as a young captain on my first staff job in the army. My commander made it clear that he wanted accurate information, even if it went against his desires. He, of course, would make the final decision, and those of us below him in the chain of command would either 'salute and execute,' or ask to be reassigned—or, in extreme cases, resign from the service. Only once in my 20-year army career was I ever told by a superior officer to 'tell me only what I want to hear,' and that officer's career, as one might imagine, came to an inglorious end not long afterwards. Not, mind you, due to anything I did, but due to his own aberrant behavior.

Secondly, this kind of activity appears to be trying to force self-censorship, the first step in the degradation of an organization's effectiveness. That it would be happening in the Department of State, the cabinet department responsible for carrying our message of respect for rule of law to the rest of the world, is an ominous sign.

An even more troubling bit of news to come my way, in July 2019, was when I was contacted by a young minority FSO who felt that in the aftermath of the president's blatant attack on four minority women members of Congress, the atmosphere in the office felt menacing. While this is not a foreign policy or diplomatic issue, it still has a potentially devastating impact on the ability of our diplomats to do their jobs.

American diplomats, indeed diplomats worldwide, work in an increasingly hostile and dangerous environment. International terrorism, transnational crime, virulent disease outbreaks, turbulent weather events, and massive dislocations of entire populations all combine to complicate their lives and endanger them and their families. When the environment at home also becomes threatening, the outlook is gloomy.

Playing with fire.

"Rebuild your world, rebuild your race, rebuild your empire. Rebuild it all. But make sure you rebuild your ideals too. Rebuild the principles that made you a great and honorable galactic power in the first place. Don't prey on the weak. Don't steal from the helpless. Don't murder the innocent. Be a force for good, not a force for yourself."
— Dan Abnett, <u>Doctor Who: The Silent Stars Go By</u>

What's the Prognosis? Will the Patient Recover?

At this point, one might expect that I would offer a prescription for the malaise that seems to be infecting American diplomacy. Indeed, I would love to be able to do just that. Unfortunately, my crystal ball is not working.

After thirty years of practicing diplomacy in foreign countries, and working the foreign policy angle in Washington, I learned the hard way that predicting the course of human events in the short term is an exercise in futility. Statistics can make fairly accurate predictions over the long term, but even over the long term, the appearance of a 'black swan," an event that deviates beyond what is normally expected to occur, and is extremely difficult to predict, throws your prediction out of whack.

At a symposium on the future of diplomacy in June 2019, I commented that the turbulence being experienced by the U.S. Foreign Service and the Department of State at the moment, while not irreversible, is likely to take several years, if not decades to mitigate. That was not a prediction, but an observation based upon more than five decades of dealing with human events. Things can be thrown out of kilter in moments, or days, but bringing them back to true takes far longer. I use the example of a house; it can be burned to the ground in a matter of minutes, but it cannot be rebuilt in the same time.

One of my fellow panelists at the symposium vehemently disagree with me, stating that we— meaning, we Americans—are resilient, and we will make a speedy recovery from the current turmoil. I chose not to argue; one, because I can't be one hundred percent certain I'm right and he's wrong, or vice versa, and two, only time will tell.

The U.S. Constitution according to Trump

"There's this thing called Article II."

Author's Note

From July 1962 to September 2012, just over half a century, I served my country, twenty years in uniform, and thirty as a diplomat. During that time, I worked for Democratic and Republican administrations, and while I did not always agree with the policies of those administrations, I had no problem carrying out the duties assigned to me to the best of my ability. When I first registered to vote in 1966 at the age of 21 (the voting age wasn't changed to 18 until 1971), I voted Republican. A native of East Texas, where the local and county governments have historically been controlled by Democrats, and having experienced extreme racial discrimination from those same Democrats, I could not bring myself to align with the Democratic Party—at the time I was not too knowledgeable of the national stance of the parties, and the rightward shift of the Republican Party wasn't apparent to me. When the Nixon strategy of appealing to the 'Silent Majority,' which I now know was just a code word for disaffected white male voters, I began to wonder. For a time, I identified as Independent, but that limited my participation in primary elections. Finally, in 2007, I realized that my personal political views aligned more closely with the Democratic Party, and since I was also living in Montgomery County, Maryland—a Democratic stronghold—I registered as a Democrat.

Having said all that, regardless of the party or candidate I supported in an election, I worked for those who were duly elected, even when the election results were called into question as they were in the 2000 elections. At times, I disagreed with certain policies for one reason or another, but never to the extent that I felt I would have to resign rather than carry them out. It was often not the overall intent of the policy I disagreed with, but the way it was intended to be carried out, or the timing. Never were my actions or responses in any way partisan, and never did I let my personal political views interfere with the performance of my duties.

Then came the 2016 elections. To say that I was shocked and saddened by the results of the election would be an understatement. There had been presidents elected before who had questionable backgrounds, or who had policy views I didn't particularly agree with. But never in my lifetime had the American voters put into office an individual who evoked a visceral reaction of dislike as they did in 2016. While I disagree with Trump's politics, what bothers me mots about him are the things that caused me to never watch his reality TV show, or to skip over articles about him in the media. I found his conduct and demeanor objectionable, his intellect questionable, and his morals nonexistent. When the reality sank in, I thanked my lucky stars that I was already retired, for if I'd not been, I would've quickly joined the ranks of those who resigned because they could not in good conscience work with or for the man.

Overnight, I became hyper-partisan, and nothing that has happened or been done since January 2017 has changed that stance, as the reader will no doubt have intuited from my use of some of my more biting editorial cartoons to illustrate this volume. So, just in case you haven't figured it out, let me be clear: I do not like Donald J. Trump, as a president or as a person. He is lacking in moral fiber and integrity, is a blatant con man and self-aggrandizer, and is totally unfit to be President of the United States. That he's a master at manipulating the media and tapping into the fears, angers, and insecurities of a large group of people, some who share his misogynistic, xenophobic views, is beyond question, but it is shockingly apparent to me that he is morally and intellectually unqualified to represent the United States of America.

I know that my views will anger that 42-46% of Americans who support the man, and will probably make even those who don't support him uncomfortable. I will not apologize for that. I only ask that these views be taken in with an open mind.

BOOKS BY THIS AUTHOR

The Adventures of Bass Reeves, Deputy U.S. Marshal

Fatal Encounter
The Marshal and the Madam
The Shaman's Curse
Renegade Roundup
Ma Barker's Boys
The Adventures of Bass Reeves, Deputy US Marshal (box set)
Bass and the Preacher
A Bad Day to Die
The Red River Queen
The Pinkerton
The Long Arm of the Law

Daniel's Journey

Wagons West: Daniel's Journey
Wagons West: Trinity: Daniel's Journey, Volume 2
Wagons West – Bounty Hunter: Daniel's Journey, Volume 3

Al Pennyback mysteries

Color Me Dead
Memorial to the Dead
Deadline
Dead, White, and Blue
A Good Day to Die
The Day the Music Died
Die, Sinner
Deadly Intentions
Death by Design

Till Death Do Us Part
Deadly Dose
Dead Man's Cove
Dead Men Don't Answer
Deadly Paradise
Kiss of Death
Death in White Satin
Death and Taxis
Deadbeat
A Deadly Wind Blows
Death Wish
Deadly Vendetta
A Time to Kill, A Time to Die
Dead Ringer
Death of Innocence
Dead Reckoning
Murder on the Menu
Over My Dead Body
Bad Girls Don't Die
A Deal to Die For
The Dead Blonde in the Red Bikini

Ed Lazenby mysteries

Butterfly Effect
Coriolis Effect
The Cat in the Hatbox
Negative Side Effects
Murder is as Easy as ABC
Body of Evidence

Buffalo Soldier series

Buffalo Soldier: Trial by Fire
Buffalo Soldier: Homecoming
Buffalo Soldier: Incident at Cactus Junction
Buffalo Soldier: Peacekeepers
Buffalo Soldier: Renegade

Buffalo Soldier: Escort Duty
Buffalo Soldier: Battle at Dead Man's Gulch
Buffalo Soldier: Yosemite
Buffalo Soldier: Comanchero
Buffalo Soldier: Range War
Buffalo Soldier: Mob Justice
Buffalo Soldier: Chasing Ghosts
Buffalo Soldier: The Piano
Buffalo Soldier: Family Feud
Buffalo Soldier: The Lost Expedition
Buffalo Soldier: The Iron Horse

Jacob Blade: Vigilante

Avenging Angel
Vengeance is Mine
Hot Lead, Cold Steel
The Vigilante From Texas
Hell in the High Country
Last Stage to Mesa Grande
Shootout at Heartbreak Ridge
A Fine Day for Dying
Vigilante League: Jacob Blade Vigilante, Books 1 - 7
Last Man Standing

Caleb Wolf Bounty Hunter series

Caleb Wolf: Date with Death
Caleb Wolf: The Missing Mail-Order Bride
Caleb Wolf: The Saga of One-Eyed jack

Other fiction

Angel on His Shoulder
She's No Angel

Child of the Flame
Pip's Revenge
Wallace in Underland
Further Adventures of Wallace in Underland
Dead Letter and Other Tales
The White Dragons
The Dragon's Lair
Dragon Slayer
The Last Gunfighters
The Culling
Frontier Justice: Bass Reeves, Deputy
  U.S. Marshal
Angel on His Shoulder-Revised Edition
Battle at the Galactic Junkyard
Mountain Man
Devil's Lake
Vixen
Awakening
Chase the Sun
The Lady's Last Song
Purgatory is the Next Stop
Catch Me if You Can
A Cowboy's Christmas Carol

Nonfiction

Things I Learned from My Grandmother About
  Leadership and Life
Taking Charge: Effective Leadership for the
  Twenty-first Century
Grab the Brass ring
African Places: A Photographic Journey
  Through Zimbabwe and southern Africa
A Portrait of Africa
There's Always a Plan B
In the Line of Fire: American Diplomats in
  the Trenches
Advice for the Insecure Writer

Looking at Life Through My Lens
Ethical Dilemmas and the Practice of Diplomacy
Making America Grate Again
DC Street Art
Dead Letters and Other Tales: Revised edition
Things I Learned From my Grandmother about
  Leadership and Life, Second Edition
Feathers, Fur, and Flowers
Backyards and Byways
American Heroes
Invasion of the Swamp Creatures

Children's books

The Yak and the Yeti
Samantha and the Bully
Molly Learns to Share
Where is Teddy?
Catie and Mister Hop-Hop
Tommy Learns to Count
Catie Goes to School

Writing as Ben Carter

William Coburn: Cowboy vs the Sea Monster

Anthologies and Collaborations

Scott Harris, U.S. Marshal
A Tribute to America's Greatest Lawmen
The Posse: A Western Adventure
Showdown at Carson's Ford: Gunfight at the River's
  Edge – with Fred Staff

ABOUT THE AUTHOR

Charles Ray has been writing fiction since his teens. He won a Sunday school magazine writing contest when he was thirteen and having his byline on a short story published in a national publication forever hooked him on writing. During his time in the army (1962-1982) he often moonlighted as a newspaper or magazine journalist and was the editorial cartoonist for the Spring Lake (NC) News, a weekly newspaper, during the 1970s. In addition to his writing, he was an artist/cartoonist and photographer for a number of publications, including Ebony, Eagle and Swan, and Essence, and had a monthly cartoon feature and did several covers for Buffalo, a now-defunct magazine that was dedicated to showcasing the contributions of African-Americans to the country's military history.

After retiring from the army, he joined the U.S. Foreign Service, and served as a diplomat in posts in Asia and Africa until his retirement in 2012. He has worked and traveled throughout the world (Antarctica is the only continent he hasn't visited), and now, as a full-time writer, continues to globetrot looking for interesting things to write about, draw, or take pictures of.

A native of Texas, he now calls Maryland home. For more on his writing and other projects, check one of the following Web sites:

http://charlesaray.blogspot.com
http://charlieray45.wordpress.com
http://www.twitter.com/charlieray45
http://www.facebook.com/charlieray45

http://www.flickr.com/photos/charlesray45/
http://www.viewbug.com/member/charlesray

You can also order some of my books through my author's website: http://charlesray-author.com/

Authors write to be read, and that can only happen when readers are made aware of the books available. Reviews are one way this happens. If you liked this book, please leave a review, even if only a few words, on Amazon or Goodreads.